Authentically You: Unveiling Your True Identity
Copyright © 2015, Yubeka Riddick

Published by BNOTCONFORMED, LLC
Phoenix, Arizona

ISBN 978-0-9967634-0-0
ISBN 978-0-9967634-1-7 (electronic)

All rights reserved. No part of this publication may be reproduced, distributed, or transmitted in any form or by any means without written permission of the publisher.

Scripture quotations marked (AMP) taken from the Amplified® Bible, Copyright © 1954, 1958, 1962, 1964, 1965, 1987 by The Lockman FoundationUsed by permission." (www.Lockman.org)

Scripture quotations marked (ESV) are from the ESV® Bible (The Holy Bible, English Standard Version®), copyright © 2001 by Crossway, a publishing ministry of Good News Publishers. Used by permission. All rights reserved."

Scripture quotations marked (ERV) taken from the HOLY BIBLE: EASY-TO-READ VERSION © 2001 by World Bible Translation Center, Inc. and used by permission.

Scripture quotations marked (KJV) are taken from the Holy Bible, King James Version (Public Domain).

All scripture used by permission. All rights reserved worldwide.

Cover Design by Riddick Agency
Editing by Darrian Tanner

Printed in the United States of America
First Edition

This book is dedicated to:

My husband, Lawrence Riddick
Thank you for being my Ephesians 3:20 (AMP)
and
Mag 6
Proverbs 27:17 (KJV)
Thank you for being my iron.

Table of Contents

Foreword   7

PART I - Identity Lost
Chapter 1   The Priceless Question   13
Chapter 2   Labels   27
Chapter 3   Expectations   41

PART II - Identity Found
Chapter 4   Searching: Finding Yourself in the Word   55
Chapter 5   Hands Up   67
Chapter 6   What Do You See?   77
Chapter 7   Saying What God Says (Say What?)   87

Part III - Identity Crisis Averted
Chapter 8   Confidence   99
Chapter 9   Rights and Benefits   109
Chapter 10   Crisis Averted   119

Prayer/Resources
Acknowledgements

Forward

Have you ever had one of those Aha moments and you wondered to yourself, who am I really? What am I really here for? Maybe you were nine, nineteen or even older when the epiphany occurred. If you were nine, then maybe it was pure excitement to be alive and you wanted the whole world to know you're here! At nineteen, you may be a tad bit more into "yourself" and anticipate others are just supposed to know who you are. But if even older, then the reality hits, you're not getting any younger, you cannot let life pass you by and not make your mark in this world. You're thinking, it's not only necessary to make it known to yourself first, but others will clearly see who you are and perhaps why you're here!

When the epiphany happened, did this thought occur: if YOU can't answer that question, it's not quite so fair to expect anyone else to answer it either. It's quite natural to seek the opinions of others, but at the end of the day, no matter what anyone says or even confirms, "you" have to be confident in who YOU are. That answer, my friend, can only come from the Creator Himself, God. If there's anyone who knows you better than you, it's God.

In this book, you will go on a journey observing how your identity begins and even how it can be lost! When it's lost, it may take your life in an unfortunate, undesirable direction. However, when your identity is discovered and not compromised, it can be a reflection of many of your personal life choices such as your relationships and personal friendships. For instance who you choose to marry, your life work or career, your purpose and other life choices should all reflect who YOU are and not what somebody else dictates who you are supposed to be. No one can give you this identity except God.

Look forward to relinquishing years of false labels and ignoring unrealistic expectations that you knowingly or unknowingly embraced. You were not born to cradle or carry either. God wants you liberated and proud to walk in your true identity only found in Him, not imposed by others.

It's exciting to know you were cut from the hand of God! Your identity was uniquely handcrafted, as a masterpiece. Not only is it important to place a priority and high value discovering who you are by God, but it also helps avoid the pitfalls and stumbling blocks of deception given to you by others.... including self-deception. Moreover, once you learn your identity is connected to God, you will discover that you have access to an exclusive VIP benefits package just because of WHO you are.

On the other hand, just in case you find yourself having a complex or identity crisis...don't worry. You will observe specific ways that are necessary to come out of that crisis. As you read along, anticipate gaining insight, doing some self-reflecting and having strategic opportunities to apply this information!

Overall, you may laugh, you may cry and you may finally have that Aha moment. The objective is to know your true identity, being convicted and confident in it without any desire to compromise or yield to a label, classification, or description that does not belong to you. So sit back, enjoy, and take this journey. YOU ARE WORTH IT!

Minister Paula Blouin
Impact Church Central Florida

PART I

IDENTITY LOST

Chapter 1
The Priceless Question

This may be one of the most commonly asked questions. It may also be the most common incorrectly answered question. Several celebrities have sat down for interviews and have been stunned by this question as they tried to find an answer. Some dates have ended because the person sitting across the table is unable to answer this question. Thousands of people 'sneak' away from the crowd to take a long look in the mirror to ask themselves this question. What question am I referring to?

Who am I?

Usually when someone asks you this question, they are trying to learn more about you. They want to know what you think of yourself. They want to know how you view yourself. The answer to this one question has the power to shape your thoughts and perspective. It also provides insight to others about who you really are. For many years, I struggled with this question.

Yubeka, who are you?

Today, I ask you that same question. The goal of this book is to help you to see yourself through the eyes of God and not through the eyes of other people.

With answering this priceless question, there are only two reactions or responses one can have. They will either respond in fear or in confidence. It is unnerving when people ask you "who are you" and you aren't sure of the answer. Your first baseline response is to state your name which is something you were taught to do since you were a toddler. However, in this case, this question takes on a different meaning. It's much deeper than that. It's something you must think about as you get older.

> **Stop trying to be someone you are not.**

Deep down inside, you must ask yourself...

Who am I?

Is your response going to be negative? Will it be positive? Will you still be in the state of trying to figure out the answer? This question plagued me for so many years because I didn't have an answer. I didn't have a response. I didn't know what to say. However, one day something changed for me. Suddenly the idea came to me that there was more to me than what I saw in the mirror. There was more to me than what other people saw when I walked into a room. I finally went to the Source, God Himself. I asked Him if He could tell me who I was. And He responded:

You are Mine.

What a great answer, but what did it mean? Your answer may be different, and that is totally fine. The only caution I give is to make sure that the answer is coming from God either through His Word or what He has spoken to your spirit. This answer was life changing; it allowed me to unveil my true identity in Christ. So I decided to dig into the Bible myself as I began this journey of finding out who I really was. I wanted to find out what He meant. I will share with you what I discovered.

Identity is defined as the set of qualities and beliefs that make a particular person or group different from others according to Merriam-Webster. In the Bible, in the book of Genesis, we find out about the creation of the world and the human race. God created Adam in His image and likeness. Adam knew and understood that he was different from all of God's other creations as he was the only one of his kind.

Authentically You

Hello Identity!! There was no struggle; there were no questions. Adam did not go around trying to be a tree, bush, or an animal. He was content as Adam, the first man. We have to learn to be content in who we are and in who God created us to be.

If you are struggling or have struggled with your identity, here is some insight. You must know and understand that you were created in the image and likeness of God!!! That's a big deal!!! Guess what? There is only one God, and there is only one you. Stop trying to be someone you are not. God does not try to be someone He isn't. He just is.

Adam had continual fellowship with God. When Eve was created, she enjoyed that same fellowship with her husband and with her Creator. God walked with them in the cool of the day. They were so confident with their image and identity that they walked around naked. Some of us can't even look in the mirror while being naked. And let's not even talk about walking around our homes while naked. I digress. They were naked, unashamed, and loving life.

Our relationship with God through Christ causes us to be naked before Him, unashamed in every area, and loving life because we live a Christ centered life. It doesn't mean that we will always get it right. It means that when we miss it, we can go to God in truth and not try to hide like Adam and Eve. When Adam and Eve made the decision to eat of the fruit of the tree of knowledge of good and evil, which signified disobedience, everything changed.

> *"And when the woman saw that the tree was good for food, and that it was pleasant to the eyes, and a tree to be desired to make one wise, she took of the fruit thereof, and did eat, and gave also unto her husband with her; and he did eat. And the eyes of them both were opened, and they knew that they were naked; and they sewed fig leaves together, and made themselves aprons.*
> *And they heard the voice of the LORD God walking in the garden in the cool of the day: and Adam and his wife hid themselves from the presence of the LORD God amongst the trees of the garden. And the LORD God called unto Adam, and said unto him, Where art thou? And he said, I heard thy voice in the garden, and I was afraid, because I was naked; and I hid myself. And he said, Who told thee that thou wast naked? Hast thou eaten of the tree, whereof I commanded thee that thou shouldest not eat?*
> *Genesis 3:6-11 (KJV)*

First, Eve saw that the tree was good for food and pleasant to the eyes. My question has always been what was wrong with the food she was currently eating? And what was she looking at in the garden that was unpleasant? How many times have we looked at something and thought it would be good for us. Maybe you don't like your nose or eyes or some other physical feature, and you seek to change it because it doesn't look the way you think it should look. God did not make a mistake in the way He designed you physically. How do I know this? Because God doesn't make mistakes. That is not His nature. Stop looking in the mirror of the world and trying to change your physical characteristics.

Now of course, not all people seek physical change for the purposes of trying to 'fit' in with the world's standard of beauty or good looks. It is different if we are trying to change some things for health reasons. After all, God want us to be healthy. In fact, in 3 John 1:2, it says that the Lord wants us to prosper even as our soul and health prospers. Part of being prosperous is to be healthy and happy with the physical characteristics that defines our looks.

No one else has the shape of your face, your eyes, your hips, lips, etc. You are a unique and original masterpiece. I love nature and how God displays His creativity through nature. My favorites are sunrises and sunsets. You will realize that no two sunsets or sunrises are the same. If God's beauty doesn't reproduce itself in nature, why would we think His beauty would reproduce itself in His children? It won't.

So man and woman knew who they were; they had continual fellowship with God. The decision that Adam and Eve made to disobey God's instructions and eat the fruit of the Tree of Knowledge of Good and Evil changed everything. It was a decision they could not undo, and it separated them from God. They were no longer sure and confident of their identity. After eating, they realized that they were naked and became ashamed, and they hid.

Unveiling Your True Identity

When we lose our identity in God, we can become like Adam and Eve, naked and ashamed. You start to question yourself. You lose sight of who you really are. The reason you feel this way is because you no longer see yourself the way God does. He sees you as beautiful and glorious. God has never had an identity crisis, and He never will. He doesn't want you to either. An identity crisis happens when you forget how you were created.

The moment Adam and Eve realized they were naked, their identity was lost. The meaning of the word lost denotes something that has been taken away or cannot be recovered; it's no longer known. There is a lack of assurance or self-confidence. So we wonder what happened to it. Eye opener here! Satan came in and took away their confidence, assurance and knowledge of who they were as God's final creation. Disobedience cost them their identity. Refusing to accept who God has created you to be is disobedience. When you look to other people to tell you who you are, you are saying to God that His thoughts don't matter. The way He sees you is no longer important. That shouldn not be.

I was talking to a friend years ago, and this question came up. We were discussing his relationship with his current partner and how he viewed himself in the context of this relationship. We were going around and around in circles. Finally, I just stopped the conversation and asked, "Who are you?" I was met with complete silence. Finally,

19

he responded, "I don't know. I'm not sure how to answer that question." Here was this 30 something year old in the middle of an identity crisis. There was no foundation. There was nothing there to support who he thought he was. There was a void, a vacuum you could say, that hadn't been filled.

After a few heartbeats of silence, my friend asked me the same question. I did not hesitate; there was no second thought required. "I am a child of the Most High God," I replied. I was confident in who I was and whose I was. And it was at that very moment that I realized my identity crisis was over, and I was finally able to answer that question without hesitation, fear or shame. I knew what God meant when He said that I was His.

> **Every relationship should speak to who you are in relation to Christ.**

Many people suffer from an identity crisis. Merriam-Webster Dictionary defines it as a feeling of unhappiness and confusion caused by not being sure about what type of person you really are or by not knowing your true purpose in life. As I stated earlier, I struggled with having an identity crisis my entire life. In looking back, those feelings of unhappiness and confusion became so overbearing that in junior high school, I thought about committing suicide. There was so much pressure from others that I couldn't take it. I just said forget it. I thought to myself if I leave today, no one would miss me. I thought that most people wouldn't even notice I was gone, and I was okay with that thought.

This is exactly what satan did to Adam and Eve in the Garden of Eden. He used suggestive thoughts to get them to lose focus off of the instructions that God gave about not eating the fruit from the Tree of Knowledge of Good and Evil. Satan is subtle and will use something as simple as a thought to get you off track. This is one of the reasons why we have to continually renew our minds.

If you are having or have had thoughts of suicide, I urge you to seek professional help. Believe me when I say that you would be missed. You have a very important part to play in this world. It is okay to reach out for help. It's important to renew your mind in the Word of God, cast down the negative thoughts that rise up, and replace them with the good thoughts from God. Remember that satan is the father of lies and there is no truth in him. So when negative thoughts come up, recognize them as the lies that they are, and say the opposite about yourself. In the African-American community, it is often seen as taboo to admit there is a need for help. This is a lie from the enemy. God created us to exist in community. You are not alone and have never been alone. Please reach out to someone.

Getting to the place of confidence in who I was in Christ was not easy. There were layers and layers of uncovering that had to take place in my life. It may be the same for you. Some people have lived for years filled with negative thoughts, emotions, unrealistic expectations, and labels that they have to get rid of. For others, it may not be that long. All it may take is changing the way you see yourself or changing what you say about yourself. Everyone's process is different because everyone has different backgrounds and things they are battling. As long as there is consistent effort and thought applied, you will see change.

When the answer to the question, "Who am I?" is found in Scripture, it changes the way we think, speak, and behave. It also changes what we allow into our lives such as the relationships we form, the jobs we take, and even the things we do for fun or pleasure. Every relationship should speak to who we are in relation to Christ.

I am not saying that we can't be friends with non-believers. Remember we are called to be salt and light in the world. We can't win others to Christ if we only exist in our limited bubble.

However, those who we are in relationship (close fellowship) with should be a reflection of who we say we are. My husband is a reflection of my thoughts about my identity. Because I believe I am a child of the Most High God, I attracted a husband who saw that in me. He treats me as such. He treats me like a child of God. He values me. My friends aren't going to ask me to do something or go somewhere that will make me question my identity as a child of the Most High God. I won't allow other people to pressure me into taking a job because of money, fame, and status, in the sense that it goes against my lifestyle as a child of the Most High God.

Once the question is answered, then our standards will align themselves to what it is we believe about ourselves. Those standards won't be compromised because they are rooted in the Word of God. I believe a lot of new believers who struggle with being fully committed to the things of God struggle because they haven't grabbed ahold of their new identity in Christ. They are struggling with the concept of reconciling the "old" them with the "new" them. In 2 Corinthians 5:17 it says

> *"Therefore, if anyone is in Christ, he is a new creation.[a] The old has passed away; behold, the new has come."* (ESV)

We have to get to the place where we hold this Scripture up to our lives like a mirror and ask ourselves, "What part of my old life am I still clinging to? What haven't I let go of now that I am in Christ?" God said that in Christ you are a new creation. New means not existing before; made, introduced, or discovered recently or now for the first time. It makes sense that we are new in Christ because before Him, we were separated from God. We are introduced to God through Christ, and now we can have a relationship with Him.

That means the answer to the question, "Who am I" is new. It's an answer that we have never heard before or even one that we did not know existed. Why? Because the answer doesn't come from our past experiences, our friends, families, or where we went to school. None of those things answer the question. The answer is based solely upon the Word of God. YAYAYAYAY! This is why I can say with confidence I am a child of the Most High God because that is what the Word says. What else does the Word say about who we are? Here are a few examples:

- We are children of God - John 1:12
- We are secure in Christ - John 10:27-29
- We are reigning in life through Jesus Christ - Romans 5:17
- We are free from condemnation - Romans 8:1
- We are complete in Christ - Colossians 2:7

These are just a few. There are so many other answers about who we are and why we were created that can be found in the Word of God. We don't have to remember them all. I encourage you to find one that speaks to you personally and make it your "go-to" answer when someone asks you the question "Who are you?" We will talk more in depth about this in Chapter 4.

Take Away
The answer to the question, "Who Am I?" can only be found in the Word of God.

Practical Application
What is one thing that I can do to begin to answer the question of "Who Am I?"

_____

_____

_____

_____

_____

_____

_____

_____

_____

_____

_____

_____

Authentically You

Chapter 2
Labels

A label is defined as a word or phrase that describes or identifies something or someone. At some point in our lives, we have all been labeled. In the world we live in, there are so many different ways to describe or identify someone. We have positive labels and negative labels. We have to decide which one we will accept. Which ones should we allow to identify us?

Some labels are a part of our natural make up. For years and even now, I've been called short and every synonym you can think of - pint size, Thumbalina, shorty, etc. I knew I was short. After a while, I started to embrace it because I knew it wasn't going to change. Thank you to my Dad for his short DNA. Former NBA star Shaquille O' Neal stands at 7'1 with a size 22 shoe. He has been labeled as the Big Aristotle. It's obvious that he's a big guy, and it will never change. So we have labels such as those which may or may not be a self image concern.

Then we have those negative labels. We hear words like stupid, ignorant, dumb, ugly, etc...the list goes on and on; I imagine many of us can add to this list with relative ease. We have all been there where someone has called us out of our name, and we are ready to fight. I was sitting in my economics class in high school, and my teacher called me a "b" in front of the entire class. Can you say 'upset'??? I wasn't just upset. I was livid. I was so angry. I knew that if I said something it was not going to be pretty. If I walked past him to get out of the classroom, I would hit him.

I sat there for the rest of the class period fuming on the inside and feeling totally and completely helpless. Even in the midst of feeling helpless, angry and upset, I made a choice not to accept that label. I did report it to his superiors. Can you even imagine how a 15 year old processes an experience like that? How about a 5 or 10 year old for that matter? Our words have power, and we have to remember this when we are ready to so quickly assign labels to others. It doesn't matter if it is a child or an adult. A label is a label and it can be assigned to anyone regardless of age, gender, or race.

There are also those labels that are attached to our personality types according to others. The labels that cross my ear gates often are the cases of being either an 'introvert' or an 'extrovert'. An introvert is defined as a shy person; a quiet person who does not find it easy to talk to other people. An extrovert is defined as a friendly person who likes to be social. An extrovert is an outgoing person. Usually a person's personality may fall into one of those two categories. Although, there are some, like myself who fit into both categories. The issue is we can grab ahold of these labels and embrace them to our detriment. If we allow it, these labels can become bondage because we feel like we have to be "this or that" when Jesus was both. He spent time away from the crowds alone with the Father, just as much as He spent time with the crowds, healing and delivering people. We have to be careful to not fall into the trap of either one.

Like some of your labels you may receive from hereditary traits, these labels may not carry a negative stigma. You can be labeled a quiet person or the life of the party. The point here is that these labels don't have to be accepted or denied. They can change. They may be a part of who we are, but they don't define who we are.

I haven't seen anywhere in the Word of God where God defines man as an introvert or extrovert. He just made man and gave instructions. During creation, God didn't breathe the breath of life into Adam and say, "I've called you to be 'shy' or I've called you to be 'comedic." God created man in His image and likeness and breathed the breath of life into him and Adam became a speaking spirit. Then God gave Adam instructions on how to live a successful life.

As I reflect on my journey, there were some labels that I embraced, and I realized later in life that I had the power to change the negative ones. And just because someone calls me a name doesn't mean I have to accept it. It doesn't even mean I have to agree with it. At the end of the day, God defines who and what I am. Not other people. Sometimes it hurts. It hurts really, really bad, and I am not making light of it at all.

One thing I've come to realize and understand about labels is that I can't be offended by the word itself. I need to look at the person who is using the words. It hurts to be called nasty names and to be put down. Nevertheless, I have grown into looking at this from a different perspective. Hurting people hurt people. When someone is hurt, they can lash out at others to cause pain because they don't know how to deal with their own pain. Sometimes, it's because they don't want to deal with the pain alone and may want someone else to join them in their pain. I'm reminded of a poem I learned in either middle school or high school. Whenever I encounter negativity such as being called a name, I just recite it.

> *Sticks and stones are hard on bones*
> *Aimed with angry art,*
> *Words can sting like anything*
> *But silence breaks the heart.*
> **– Phyllis McGinley**

This poem reinforces that words have power. Words can invoke feelings of hurt, joy, love, or pain. Our words are important, and we need to be careful with how we use them.

There is nothing quite like silence. Silence isn't always seen as a weakness. There is strength in learning how to use words or even to not use words. How much power is there in the person who chooses to walk away from a negative confrontation? There is tremendous power in learning how not to stoop to the level of a bully.

However, in the silence, you have to be careful not to accept the words being hurled at you like stick and stones. Physical bruises fade, but the bruises left upon our heart can take years to heal. God, the Great Physician, has the power to heal the bruises left by the negative names and labels we've been called. The key to healing is allowing God in. He is a Master Surgeon, who with great precision, can skillfully mend our hearts. In Luke 4:18, it tells us that Jesus came to heal the brokenhearted.

It's amazing to me that God knew in advance that we would need our hearts to be healed; it became one of the assignments of Jesus. If you are still dealing with the negative labels that people have tried to throw on you, I encourage you to find a quiet place and allow the Master Surgeon to perform open heart surgery. It will hurt, but after surgery is done, your heart will be stronger.

We've talked about the negative labels we've been assigned by others. What about the ones we've assigned ourselves? I understand that the names we call ourselves can stem from the labels we were given by others. It gets to a point where we have rehearsed those names for so long that they are now a part of who we are.

When we have spent years hearing that we aren't good enough, or smart enough, or whatever enough, it can erode our self-esteem. We have now internalized these negative labels to the point that we have allowed those words to become our reality. This can surely happen if we don't renew our minds by saying what God has said about us.

I was the kid who was smart, but not quite smart enough. I was in the gifted and talented program from 1st grade until High School, with the exception of the 5th grade when I got bored. At the time, I didn't know I was bored and so I had a very lackadaisical attitude about school. It was only when I was in college that I figured out how my brain worked. I started to understand my learning process.

When I applied to get into certain middle schools, I was told I wasn't smart enough to get into this particular program. The passing grade was 80 percent for every class. My mom fought and assured the administrators that I could indeed succeed and do well. I proved them wrong by passing all of my classes with an 80% or higher. There were a few classes in which I received a 75%, but I showed them that I would not be labeled.

In 7th and 8th grade, you don't particularly care about grades. At least I didn't. I cared about fitting in and having friends. My grades didn't suffer because of it, but I had always felt awkward. It was something that I personally had to get over, but that didn't happen until years later.

Because of the grades I received, I was a nerd. My mom enforced the 80% passing grade in high school. Imagine my look of confusion knowing that the passing grade in my High School was 65% but my mother expected me to bring home 80% and above. The standard was set and I could not deviate from it. I have always said that children will live up to the standard that's set for them. So, now I'm being called a nerd. I was told that I "talked white". I had no idea what this meant until I realized it was because I spoke proper English.

Those years were particularly rough because I found myself doing things that went against my standards in order to not be labeled something negative. I wanted to be cool. I considered myself a "cool nerd". I had great friends and wasn't socially awkward. But I still carried around those negative labels and names even when I became an adult.

Your story may not be my story or it may be similar. What are the negative labels you have embraced and made your own? Have you accepted the package like I did? I'm talking about the package of names and labels. I didn't just accept the package, I opened it up and allowed it to reside in my heart and in my mind. The Bible tells us that God knows us down to the very number of hairs on our head, even when we don't know ourselves.

We have to take stock and do some internal evaluation of what we believe about ourselves. We have to figure out the root of our beliefs. Did it come from others? Did it come from ourselves? Did it come from God? God desires for His children to get a full and complete understanding of who we are from His Word. Your identity, my identity, our identity cannot be found outside of our relationship with Christ. Anyone who says differently is lying. Yes, I said it, and yes I mean it. As a new creation in Christ, we have a new identity. We have new DNA. It's just not our spirit that has been recreated, but our DNA has been recreated to reflect the DNA of our Heavenly Father.

> **One of the greatest threats to the enemy is a child of God who knows his or her identity.**

The enemy will do all he can to bring those negative names and labels to the forefront of our thinking. Why? Because one of the greatest threats to the enemy is a child of God who knows his or her identity.

As long as he can keep us wrapped up in thinking we aren't good enough, he doesn't have to worry about us doing anything great for the kingdom of God. Why? Because WE won't think we can do anything great for the Kingdom. It doesn't matter how many times God has told us we are called to greatness. It doesn't matter how many times we are told we are called to greatness by others. If we don't think we are, we won't be great.

We can only be great to the extent that we believe it. Greatness isn't something that we get to 'do'. Our greatness is rooted in our Heavenly DNA. We are great because God is great, and we are His children. Negative labels have never stopped the plan of God. Look at Rahab, a prostitute who is in the lineage of Christ. Do you think that God looked at the fact that she was called a prostitute and said that she can never be included in the lineage of Christ? No, God looked at her and said that He would use her to save His people. As a result, she was saved and included in the lineage of Christ. I don't know the stigma she endured during Biblical times; however, I imagine it wasn't pleasant.

We can't focus on the things we have been called. We can't look back at our past challenges when there is so much more God has for us. We have to make a choice to accept what God has said about us. There isn't anyone else who can make that decision.

The decisions we make each day are the steps we walk in tomorrow. We have two choices. We can decide to continue to rehearse the negative identities that have been ascribed to us and let them paralyze us from moving forward in our assignment. Or we can reject those labels and rehearse what God continually says about us in His Word and move forward in faith towards completing our assignment.

It's easy to get stuck in the past or in the present when there isn't a clear understanding of who you are and what you are called to do. However, don't let that stop you from taking the necessary steps no matter how small they may seem. Fear gets to the edge of the cliff and says 'what if', while faith takes a flying leap and says 'God's got this'.

We can't leap in faith when the weights and chains of names and labels are holding us to the ground. It's time to say NO MORE!! Refuse to be identified by a label that does not reflect your Heavenly Father. Remember we are one decision away from having freedom.

The positive labels we have been ascribed in life also need to be held up to the Word of God. Just because a word seems positive doesn't mean it can't be distorted. For example, if you continuously tell a child that she is beautiful and excuse ugly behavior, then that child may grow up thinking her looks are all that matter. If you consistently tell people that they are smart and excuse their arrogance, they may grow up to be prideful.

It is important that we have balance when using and choosing our words. The words we use today are seeds that are planted in the hearts of people. They will return a harvest. We have to be prepared for the harvest when it comes. Pastor David Blouin of Impact Church Central Florida said "Words are like automobiles, they are on a pathway to collide with someone's heart. Be careful that they don't cause accidents."

As we take a moment and reflect on the positive and negative labels that have tried to attach themselves to our lives, remember to hold them up to the mirror of the Word. The Word of God is our final authority in everything we say and do.

We must let go of the labels that don't align with God's purpose for our life. Forget the labels that don't measure up to where we see ourselves. We must allow Jesus to heal our broken hearts. Again, I'm not saying it is easy. There will be tears, anger, frustration, and hurt. It is only when the ground is broken that the foundation can be poured. We have to trust that God will root out everything that should not be there and plant everything we need to fulfill our purpose on this earth.

Take Away
Both negative and positive labels need to be held up to the Word of God. I get to decide if I will accept or reject the package.

Practical Application
What labels and names do you need to get rid of in order to embrace your God-given identity?

_____
_____
_____
_____
_____
_____
_____
_____
_____
_____
_____
_____
_____

Unveiling Your True Identity

Authentically You

Chapter 3
Expectations

Expectations are hard to live up to, whether they are self-imposed or imposed by others. Expectation is defined as a belief that something will happen or is likely to happen; a feeling or belief about how successful, or good someone or something will be. At what point in time do we think about God's expectations? Where is He in the grand scheme of things? The frightening truth is that we seldom take the time to think about what God expects or wants us to do. There are times when He isn't even a part of the equation. We shut out His thoughts, plans, and purpose for our lives and don't pause to give it a second thought. Then when we are frustrated, we pray for grace to finish an assignment that we decided to pick up by our own will.

We are expected to be good workers, employers, employees, servers, moms, daughters, sisters, and friends. The list can go on and on and on. These are called roles. Of course, we want to be great friends and wives and mothers and daughters. However, our roles don't define us either. Let's stop and think about this for a second. What if we take all of those expectations and put them down and cast them to the side? What are we left with? Just ourselves. Is it difficult to define yourself outside of all of these expectations and roles? I don't know who I am because I can't be anyone except who people "expect" me to be. What kind of nonsense is that? It's time for an examination of who we really are outside of the lines and boundaries that we have drawn or have allowed others to draw for us. This is how we lose our true identity.

We have allowed society to place these expectations on us, and we have pushed God's expectations to the back burner. We have this idea that God will be fine with us being who we are not as long as we serve and live for Him 'sometimes'. That's crazy. God doesn't want us to go around fulfilling and living up to the expectations of others, especially not those of the world. He wants us to live according to His Word.

> **We have unconsciously taken on other people's expectations and have locked ourselves in a self-imposed prison.**

There comes a point in life when all of that pressure will become too much. Then we cry out to God to help us by taking it away. And His response will be that He never gave it to us in the first place. He tells us to stop trying to be someone we are not because that is not who He has created us to be. (An Aha moment.)

Lord, what do you mean? We unwittingly take on these roles in the hopes that we are pleasing God by pleasing other people only to find out we have placed ourselves in bondage. We aren't free. We aren't free to be the person who laughs out loud, tells funny jokes, snorts in public, or whatever it may be.

We have unconsciously taken on other people's expectations and have locked ourselves in a self-imposed prison. Now is the time to get free and stay free. Public opinion can be so restrictive and confined. It's one of the masks that we can put on daily. It's called the mask of public opinion. On the outside we are who people want us to be, but on the inside the real us is crying to break free. How much does it hurt God when we aren't true to ourselves?

Can you imagine the mountains saying today that I am going to put on the mask of the sea because that is what everyone wants me to be? We will look at that statement and think it's crazy. Where does God get the glory when the mountain decides it wants to be something else? He doesn't. The same is true for you and me. God doesn't get the glory when we pretend to be something we are not because it is what is expected of us.

It's time for the lies to stop and for freedom from public opinion to be loosed. Now, let me just say this does not mean that you get to go around telling people whatever you want in the name of being free from public opinion. What it means is that you are free to be who you are in the face of what the Word says and to be comfortable in the skin you are in. Remember God is still a God of decency and order. So don't go around telling folks that Yubeka said that I can do and say anything I want because I am free from public opinion. Nope, I didn't say that, and I will not co-sign on it either.

In Corinthians 12, Paul talks about the parts of the Body. Every part is important, and every part is necessary. He reminds the church of this. We have to remember that whatever part we play in the Body of Christ, God has specifically assigned it to us. We cannot get caught up in trying to be a part of the body that we were not assigned to. This is where we can have unrealistic expectations. We have the expectation of being the "foot" when God has created us to be a "hand" We walk around frustrated because we don't feel like we are accomplishing anything or we aren't contributing to the Kingdom. It's not that we aren't accomplishing anything. It's that we are not in our lane. We have gotten caught up in being something we are not.

But as it is, God has placed and arranged the limbs and organs in the body, each [particular one] of them, just as He wished and saw fit and with the best adaptation."
1 Corinthians 12:18 (AMP)

We have been arranged in the Body of Christ as God has seen fit. We have been fashioned and ordered according to God's plan. So, when someone tries to make us into something we are not by imposing expectations, we can reject them with confidence. It's not that we don't want the help. It's just that we must ask ourselves is this what God is expecting of us. Are we in the place that God has called us to be or are we trying to be something we aren't at the expense of our mental, spiritual, and emotional health? Are we more concerned with pleasing others than we are with pleasing God? These are all questions we must ask ourselves when we are asked to live up to unrealistic expectations.

When I first got married, I "thought" my husband had this expectation that I would cook for him every day. We have all heard of the Proverbs 31 woman. To be totally honest, this woman makes me exhausted. I mean she did everything and then some. She did so much that she is brandished about in Christian circles as the model woman. Let's be honest, how many of us are trying to be this Proverbs 31 woman? Yes, I was as well.

Then I came into realization that I was placing all of these unrealistic expectations on myself. My husband didn't expect me to be her. He expected me to be Yubeka, period. The Bible tells us that it is unwise to for us compare ourselves amongst other people. I would like to think that this is true for comparing ourselves to the Proverbs 31 woman. There are so many different characteristics we can learn from her without trying to be her. At the end of the day, the only person we are taught to pattern our lives after is Jesus. The last time I checked my Bible, the Proverbs 31 woman was not Jesus.

We will get set free from the unrealistic expectations we set for ourselves. So back to my cooking dinner every night. There were some nights where I was just physically exhausted and the thought of making dinner was not at the top of my list. I would do it anyway. One day I had so many moving pieces that needed to get done once I got off of work it was overwhelming. My husband stepped in and offered to cook dinner and run errands so that I could get everything done. He asked me why I didn't ask him for help. I didn't have a valid reason for not asking him. In that moment, I recognized the grace that God has sent to me through my husband. After a conversation where I expressed my frustration with not living up to be the "perfect wife" by cooking, he responded with, "I didn't and I don't expect you to cook all of the time. I can help you. We are a team."

It was one of my first Aha! Moments in my marriage. I had placed this expectation on myself. My husband had no idea this was going on in my head. Once I communicated my frustrations and this expectation, I was instantly set free with his response.

Unveiling Your True Identity

Sometimes it only takes communicating with others about certain expectations. When we stay in bondage, we are operating in our flesh and expecting God to provide grace. We get upset when the grace isn't manifested. We have to remember that it isn't manifested because this isn't something God has told us to do. We've taken on all of this extra responsibility for many different reasons and the most important reason has not even been a factor.

Unrealistic expectations can be one of the greatest hindrances to us embracing our true identity. We can impose these expectations that force us to be "Superwoman" when in actuality, we are stopping God from being God in our lives. We figure that we have to be perfect. We have to work outside the home. We have to be a stay at home mom or whatever the case may be. We can place these expectations on ourselves or we can have them placed there from others. Sometimes it's not a matter of how other people view us: it's about how we view ourselves in light of what other people have and what other people do. Stop it. Stop it right now. What good will come if you try to compare your actions and possessions to those of others? Absolutely nothing. There is nothing good that will come from it.

We have to find out what God expects from us. What does the Bible say about expectations? Does God want me to try to be everything to everyone? Or should I be focusing on how to be the best at one thing? Maybe you should focus on relationships. Maybe

God is instructing you to focus on finances. It could be something simple as working on the Fruit of the Spirit (love, joy, peace, meekness, longsuffering.....Gal 5:22) Whatever it is, that is what you should focus on. This is where God is expecting growth and improvement.

We can get lost in the maze of trying to figure out whose expectations to meet first. After a while, that becomes exhausting. Paul said that he became all things to all people, but guess what... Paul had the grace to do that. If God has given you the grace, have at it. If not, you will become exhausted very quickly trying to live up to others' expectations. It doesn't matter if they are realistic or not.

I tell people all of the time that my husband and I are two imperfect people trying to love each other perfectly. Will we miss it sometimes? Absolutely. But the point is that we recognize that there may be times where we place unrealistic expectations on ourselves and each other. When that happens, we have to communicate effectively about how we are feeling and why we are feeling that way. It invariably comes down to both of us saying to each other, "Honey, I didn't expect you to do that and you don't have to." Talk about a weight off of each other's shoulders.

This may require a tough conversation between you and someone else about how you are feeling. Be honest, and do not feel bad for wanting to communicate how you are feeling in that moment. Don't get discouraged if at first it seems as if the expectation hasn't gone anywhere. Ultimately, when you start focusing on what God wants, others will notice and follow suit.

Take Away
I have the grace to do and be exactly who God created me to be.

Practical Application
What are some unrealistic expectations you impose on yourself and others that may hinder your growth in Christ?

_____

_____

_____

_____

_____

_____

_____

_____

_____

_____

_____

_____

Unveiling Your True Identity

PART II
IDENTITY FOUND

Authentically You

Chapter 4
Searching: Finding Yourself in the Word

In Chapter 1, I talked about the foundational result of you finding yourself in the Word. In this chapter, we take it a bit further. We have all heard the phrase, "I need to find myself." Usually, we envision a person traveling around the world without a thought or care. For others, it may mean living on a beach with the wind blowing and the sun shining down upon you. Whatever you envision when you hear that phrase, if it does not signify getting closer to God through Christ, you have just taken a long journey to the Land of Nowhere.

Finding ourselves should always start with the Word of God. The best example of this is Jesus. Before Jesus began His ministry, He was baptized in the Jordan River by John the Baptist and was full of the Holy Spirit. Immediately afterwards, He was tempted in the wilderness by satan after having fasted for forty days and forty nights.

During the temptation by satan, Jesus referred to the Word of God in response to the temptation. Jesus had to know who He was in order to resist the temptation presented by the devil.

When we know who we are based upon the Word, we are able to resist the temptation presented by the devil, just like Jesus. After Jesus used the Word to resist temptation, He went into the temple and read from the book of Isaiah. He read the purpose of His ministry here on the earth. After He finished reading He closed the book and stated, "This day is this scripture fulfilled in your ears." (Luke 4:21 KJV)

Jesus knew that He was one hundred percent man and one hundred percent God. Even with this knowledge and understanding, He found Himself in the Word of God. As children of God, we also have to find ourselves in the Word. What does this mean? I'm glad you asked. When we struggle with understanding who we are and why we are here, we have to go to God. The best way to do that outside of prayer is by reading the Word.

Within the Word of God, we can find our purpose. We find other people who battle with some of the same issues we face. We find hope. We find joy. We find solutions. Just as Jesus went to the Word at the beginning of His ministry, we need to do the same. He identified Himself in the Word and recognized it as His divine assignment. He never questioned His identity or His assignment. Throughout scripture, He constantly reaffirmed that He was the Messiah, and He knew His purpose for coming to earth.

Our true identity is found in relationship with Christ as stated earlier. I remember when I was in the midst of my own identity crisis. At 25, I was trying to find myself, and I was learning how to be happy with who God created me to be. This journey started with me moving across the country from Brooklyn, NY to Phoenix, AZ. I moved by faith, without a job and trusting that God had something for me in Phoenix. It was hard to leave my family and friends; however, I knew that if I wanted more out of life, I couldn't obtain it living in New York. The stress and pressure that came from the unrealistic expectations became too much, and I no longer knew who I was or who God created me to be.

> **For every new season in our lives, we learn something different about ourselves.**

Within two months of arriving in Phoenix, I had a job and a new church family, but most importantly, I had the space to develop a true relationship with Jesus Christ. My driver's license didn't come until seven months later, but hey, I'm a New Yorker. I thought with the move, I would only have to go through this one time in my life. Unfortunately, that wasn't the case.

For every new season in our lives, we learn something different about ourselves. It has been said that seasons change once purpose has been fulfilled. One of the purposes for any season in our life is to gain a better understanding of who we are. For example, as a single person, I had to learn how to be content with who I was. I had to enjoy being in my own company. When I got married, I had to learn how to love selflessly, share my space and how to compromise on something as small as what to eat for dinner. Talk about an adjustment. I couldn't just make decisions for myself and by myself, there was someone else's thoughts, opinions, and ideas that I had to consider, my husband's. Here was a new piece of my identity that I had to learn and become comfortable with. If you feel like you are "stuck" in a particular season, ask Holy Spirit to reveal the part of your identity you need for the next season.

It's like a puzzle. Each piece of that puzzle ultimately creates a whole person. In every puzzle, you have the background, the one with the most pieces or the most dominant color. Those pieces make up the foundation of the puzzle, and everything else is built around that foundation. The same can be said as we discover our identity. We discover the pieces that make up who we are. The most important piece to the puzzle of our lives is the foundation, and that foundation is the Word of God. That should be the biggest piece.

The Word of God has the solution to every question we may ever have about ourselves. My pastor once said that if you want to know how and why something was created, go to the source. Go to the one who created it. Trying to find our identity without going to God is like taking the pieces from one puzzle and trying to fit those pieces into a different one. It won't work. We have to go back to the source or in the case of a puzzle, the picture on the box.

When people questioned Jesus about who He was, He always referred back to the Father. When we are asked the priceless question from Chapter One, do we refer back to the Word or do we answer with our own mind and understanding? Are we still defining ourselves by our physical traits? By what others have said? Or even by what we think?

Our mind and understanding are subject to our circumstances and situations. This is why we are told to renew our minds in Romans 12:2. The renewing of our minds isn't something that only happens once. Renewing our minds is a daily process. Thoughts pop into our heads on a consistent basis; however, all of these thoughts are not from God. Sometimes they are our own based upon our experiences, and sometimes they are from the enemy.

The best way to find out if a thought is from God is to hold it up to the mirror of the Word. Does this thought line up with Scripture?

A great example of this is when we say, "I'm losing my mind." This thought does not line up with the Word. In 1 Corinthians 1:10 it says we have the mind of Christ and Christ has never lost His mind. This is one way that we keep our minds from going tilt.

Jesus was confident in His assignment, His purpose, and His mission. There were many times throughout the scripture where He had to remind His disciples and others of His identity.

In Matthew 16:13-18, Jesus asks His disciples

"...Whom do men say that I the Son of man am? And they said, Some say that thou art John the Baptist: some, Elias; and others Jeremias, or one of the prophets. He saith unto them, But whom say ye that I am? And Simon Peter answered and said Thou art the Christ, the Son of the living God." (KJV)

We know that Jesus never asks a question that He doesn't already know the answer to. So, in this Scripture, He wants to find out what other people are saying about him. He then asks the disciples who do they say He is. He never questioned His own identity. When the disciples told Him who other people thought He was, He neither confirmed nor denied it.

> **Finding ourselves in the Word of God doesn't happen overnight.**

He didn't have to justify if He was the Son of the Living God. He didn't pause to give an explanation. He then turned around and asked the disciples, who had been with Him, who did they say He was. Peter's response blessed Him because Jesus knew the revelation Peter received came from God.

When was the last time you received a revelation about who Jesus was from God? How does that revelation help you understand your own identity in Christ? Every situation and circumstance that we face as Christians should come with a greater understanding of who we are in Christ.

Finding ourselves in the Word of God doesn't happen overnight. It may be that during different seasons we identify with different characters. The first time I found myself in the Word was in the story of Jacob. Now, originally when I saw that it was Jacob, I had a moment of confusion. Why? First, I am not a man. Second, I am not a liar. Third, I am not a trickster. I could have shut down the revelation that God wanted me to get, but I persevered. What did God want me to get from Jacob's story?

One of the most important things I realized in identifying with Jacob was he had to establish his own relationship with God. His relationship could not be based upon his father or grandfather's. I grew up in the church. My grandmother is an Evangelist, and my mother rededicated her life to Christ and has served God since her rededication. In some ways, I lived my Christian life through them. Because of my background, I could relate to Jacob's struggle of coming to know God for himself. It took him leaving his family in search of a wife to come to know God.

I did leave my family in New York in 2003 and embarked upon a relationship to get to know God for myself outside of the external influences, labels, and expectations of my family and friends. I found myself in the Word through study, prayer, and serving in my church. I haven't been the same since. It was during this time I learned how to be happy with myself, the Yubeka that God created. I found my purpose and God's assignment for my life. So much so, I ended up in Florida 5 years later to attend Bible School. When was the last time you found yourself in the Word?

Through the Word, we can be directed towards certain characteristics God wants us to focus on through the biblical characters. The key is allowing ourselves time to read the story, recognize the lessons, and identify what revelation God is trying to give us. Once we answer those questions, we get another piece of the puzzle.

Pieces of our identity will be lost as long as we refuse to find ourselves in Scripture. It's never easy to look at ourselves and realize

God wants us to make adjustments. We can get upset, angry, become stubborn and say we aren't making any changes. But who loses when this happens? Not God. We do. Other people are affected by our decision to remain the way we are. These can be people assigned to us meaning we are to positively influence and inspire them during our journey. These are people who are waiting on us. We shortchange the power of God to make lasting and effective changes in their lives.

Stubbornness will keep you out of the perfect will of God. The perfect will of God is His Word. No more, no less. Sacrificing our old selves to become new in Christ is not a sacrifice at all. Jesus endured the cross that was set before Him because He saw us at the end of the torture and the abuse. Imagine if Jesus would have never found Himself in scripture. Imagine if He would have never read the book of Isaiah? Imagine if He would have never found His crucifixion in the Word? Would He have endured the cross as well as He did? I don't know, but I am apt to believe that knowing this was coming helped to endure the shame, the guilt, and the sin of man. God isn't asking us to endure the cross and the sins of the entire world. Whatever God may ask us to endure or face, He has already provided a way to overcome. The answer is found in His Word.

> **Pieces of our identity will be lost as long as we refuse to find ourselves in Scripture.**

When we don't understand some of the challenges and obstacles we may go through, we can always look in the Word. In the book of Ecclesiastes, it says there is nothing new under the sun. This reinforces that other people have dealt with some of the same issues and challenges. If we never find out how they overcame them, we can end up like the foolish woman in Proverbs who has to experience life in order to learn lessons versus the wise woman who observed from a distance and made the adjustment without the experience.

Take Away
Finding myself in the Word of God is vitally important to unveiling the real me.

Practical Application
Pray and ask God to reveal who you are in His Word and write down the characteristics that bear witness with you.

_____

_____

_____

_____

_____

_____

_____

_____

_____

_____

_____

_____

_____

Authentically You

Chapter 5
Hands Up

We previously discussed how our identity was lost through sin and how it was found through the Cross. We will discuss the three ways we claim our identity once we have found ourselves in the Word.

The first way is by submitting your thoughts to the Word of God. The second is choosing to see ourselves the way God sees us. The third way is to say what God says about us continuously. These three things combined will help us to prevent or ward off an undesirable occurrence and assist us in turning our eyes and thoughts away from the lies of the enemy.

The first one we will discuss is submission. I know no one wants to talk about submission particularly in the church or even outside of the church. The word submission can cause an immediate panic attack. Even worse, it can cause someone to shut down. Stay with me as we discuss the taboo "s-word".

Submission is defined as the action or fact of accepting or yielding to a superior force or to the will or authority of another person according to Merriam-Webster Dictionary. For our purposes, the person we are submitting to is God. I've always wondered why it was so difficult for people, myself included, to submit to God, especially knowing His character. I think it comes from growing up in a society where independence is taught as a means of success. What I mean by that is people don't believe in their heart that they need anyone for anything. However, this is a lie. We were created to exist in community. Adam and Eve existed in community; one of the largest parts of that community was habitual fellowship with God.

When we have habitual fellowship with God, we understand that His thoughts are higher than our thoughts and His ways are higher than our ways. It puts submission in a different context. For most of our lives, we have lived outside of submission to God. It may not be every part of our lives, but when we don't see ourselves the way God sees us, that is disobedience.

I remember one Sunday at church, my pastor was preaching a message and I was NOT trying to submit to God's plans for my life. This had been an ongoing struggle for three months straight because in the natural, I did not want to accept it. Every time the subject came up in prayer, I would tell God "No, that isn't something I want to do." In my mind and heart, I was perfectly okay with saying no. At least that is what I thought. So we get to this Sunday (I don't remember the message), and my Pastor makes one of many comments during the message that hit me right where it hurts.

Unveiling Your True Identity

He said, "You can't tell the Creator that He created you incorrectly". That is exactly what I was doing. I cried throughout the entire service. I'm not talking about the sniffles. I'm talking about the ugly cry. During the entire service, I realized that I needed to repent and submit to what God was telling me about myself and about my purpose. When we submit to what God says about us, it is very difficult for someone to come in and tell us anything differently. When we know our identity, we identify our standards.

Our standards, as children of God, should come from God and His Word. I know we've heard the saying "If you don't stand for something, you'll fall for anything." A lot of pain, hurt, anger, and low self-esteem issues come from not having morals and standards. You have to stand for something, and that something is your identity. It makes it easy for us to give in to temptation, pressure, and lies when we do otherwise.

> **When we know our identity, we identify our standards.**

Submission is not always the first thing we think about when it comes to our identity but it should be. So what does this look like? Great question. We talked about labels and expectations earlier. It is taking all of those labels and expectations one by one and holding them up to the mirror of the Word. I'll give you an example. One of the expectations that I dealt with was having to be perfect. I didn't realize it was an unrealistic and unattainable goal until I was 25.

I struggled with the desire to not disappoint people who meant a lot to me. I had to do and be "good" all the time. I didn't want to rock the boat; I managed to stay under the radar with people. Finally, I had a "come to Jesus" moment when I realized I was not Jesus, and I would eventually hurt someone. I was not perfect, and I didn't have to try to be perfect. Perfection as a believer is not something we will ever attain while here on earth. I came to the realization that there was one perfect person on earth...Christ. God did not create me to be Christ. Instead, He admonishes us to be followers of Christ.

Have you dealt with any of the unrealistic expectations that you have placed on yourself? Once we realize with confidence that we can't be anyone besides who God has designed us to be, we are truly free. Where the Spirit of the Lord is, there is liberty. There is a true freedom when Holy Spirit dwells within us.

We have to rid ourselves of public opinion and what people may think about us. My husband and I were in a bookstore purchasing a book for a friend. I went to stand in the line. I followed the sign that said, "Enter here". There were some people who decided to make their own line. A gentleman walked up to the line and proceeded to get in the line with the people who created their own line. My husband walks up and asks me why was I standing at that particular spot. My response was I know how to follow instructions. I told him God is not a God of chaos and I am not a goat but a sheep.

Little did I know the gentleman who was "technically" behind me heard every word I said. Later that evening my husband informed me the gentleman turned red. I didn't mean to embarrass him. However, I was confident in who I was to not be moved by what other people were doing. I am sure I looked quite odd as I was the only person "standing in line". At any point the gentleman could have walked up and stood behind me, but he chose to follow everyone else. How often do we dare to be different? It's not that we are trying to prove a point, but it's about us being confident in who we are. We serve a God of decency and order. We don't get to make our own rules and then wonder why everything is disorganized.

Public opinion is a form of bondage God has freed us from. Oftentimes, we are so much more concerned with what others think than we are with what God not only thinks, but with what He has said about us. There are times when we are disobedient to God because we fear what others have said or what they may say.

Today is the day we become free from public opinion. No one has a heaven or hell to put us in. When it comes down to it, we live for the approval of one. You make a great 'you' and a lousy 'someone else', so why would you even try? God knew what He was doing when

He created us. He didn't create us to look or be like anyone else. He created us in His image and likeness. God has many different facets that make up who He is. Remember, the angels circle the throne crying "Holy, Holy, Holy". Each time they revolve around the throne, they see a different facet of God. Why would His creation be any different? When we embrace our God-given identity, we reflect a different facet of God.

We have faith in who we are in Christ by submitting to His Word. We don't submit to His Word because it's the "easy" thing to do. We submit because it shows how much we love Him. He takes the hot mess that we are and cleans us up to reflect Him when we decide to submit to what He says about us. The decision to submit is totally up to us. His word is finite. It doesn't change and hasn't changed since it was written. However, how we choose to apply the Word determines whether we avert an identity crisis.

> **Today is the day we become free from public opinion.**

To decide to not submit to the Word regarding our identity is rooted in pride. Pride says, "Not only do I not have to submit to the Word, I don't even believe the Word when it comes to who God created me to be." If we can believe the Word for salvation, the gift of Holy Spirit, healing, increase in our finances, etc., why can't we believe the Word when it comes to our identity?

Why is it easier to believe other people who may or may not have our best interest at heart than it is to believe God? We are so quick to grab ahold of the message of "prosperity", "healing", "grace", "freedom", but we are reluctant to grab ahold of our true identity. The benefits that we have access to as children of God come to us when we know and take a firm hold of who we are in Him. Notice the Bible calls us sons of God and joint heirs with Christ; this is our identity. But what do you call yourself, and do you believe it?

Maybe we have a difficult time submitting to the Word because we haven't embraced who we are in Christ. When we don't submit, we limit our access to the benefits that come from being a child of God. We hold on to the "old" us and selfishly think that we don't have to change what we think about ourselves. Proverbs 16:18 says that "Pride goes before destruction, and a haughty spirit before a fall." The root of an identity crises is pride and selfishness.

There comes a point where we will be forced to look at ourselves in the mirror of the Word and make a decision about who we are and what we will submit to God. Will we surrender all, including but not limited to our thinking about ourselves? Or will we continue to hold that part of ourselves back and miss out on the freedom that lies in Christ?

Take Away

Submitting to the Word about who I am is my decision. It is a decision I may have to make on a daily basis.

Practical Application

What is one area about me that I can submit to the Word? What is my foundation scripture? What can I do daily to submit in this area to God?

_____
_____
_____
_____
_____
_____
_____
_____
_____
_____
_____
_____
_____

Unveiling Your True Identity

Chapter 6
What Do You See?

Now once you submit your thoughts to God, you must do the next step. The second step in claiming our identity is learning how to see ourselves through the lens of the Word and not the lens of the World. The word 'see' is defined by Merriam Webster as to perceive with the eyes; discern visually; discern or deduce mentally after reflection or from information; understand.

In this age, cameras are everywhere. You can take a picture at any time and anywhere right from your cell phone. In general, cameras have lenses. There may be times when we need to change the lens to accurately capture the subject of the picture.

It may be challenging to figure out which lens we are using when taking a picture. One day, we purchase a new lens for our camera and we can't wait to start "clicking" away. When we look through the lens everything looks great. The lens is a little cumbersome, but it's okay. Our pictures are going to be great. The sticker says "satisfaction guaranteed". The subject is in focus and centered on the screen. There is enough light. The picture is balanced and "click", we take the picture.

Sometimes, we don't even check to make sure all of the 'ingredients' that make a great picture are there. We just click, keep moving and start posting to social media. And what we don't realize is that our lens is flawed. It was created to make it seem like everything is great and picture perfect. Remember the sticker. There are no adjustments that need to be made, and we can continue to click and go on with life as usual. There are no bad shots with this lens; there are no flaws. We don't need to go back and make any edits. We are fine just the way we are.

Then one day, we get a new lens. The sticker said 'free', but it may require some additional work. We jumped on the offer. This lens is lighter and easier. We start taking pictures with our new lens and realize we are going to have to do some work. We look at the subject of our photo and realize, uh oh... we need to adjust the focus. The subject is blurry and not centered. The balance is off. The lighting is all wrong and needs to be adjusted. We realize that we will have to spend some time editing our shots.

The subject of our pictures are our identities. With the first lens, our identity is fine. We are focused, and everything is balanced. There is enough light, and guess what? Our satisfaction is guaranteed, and we don't ever have to make adjustments. Sounds too good to be true? It is. When we view our identity through the lens of the world, it will lie to us all day and every day. It will continue to tell us day after day that everything is fine. We can go on with our life as usual without making any adjustments. Even though this lens is cumbersome, we continue to use it because it gives us a false sense of who we are and makes us feel good about it.

The lens that's lighter and easier to use comes with a disclaimer. Even though it's free, there will be work involved. Our subject of the picture hasn't changed with this new lens. However, our view of our identity when we look through this lens is a true reflection of who we are. With this lens, we have to focus our identity within the shot. It's really blurry, but the lens is great for getting everything in focus. The shot isn't balanced, and there are some shadows that show up in this view. At first, we are okay with working with this new lens, but after a while we get tired because the work that we need to put in to get a good shot is just too much.

The second lens is the lens of the Word. When we find Scripture that confirms who we are, it's like 'focusing' the subject. The Word has the ability to bring our identity into focus and balance everything around us.

There may be times when we don't have enough light and the subject we are viewing (our identity) has shadows, or it may be dark. When we view identity through the lens, then the Word will shine light in the darkness and get rid of the shadows.

In the beginning was the Word, and the Word was with God, and the Word was God. The same was in the beginning with God. All things were made by him; and without him was not anything made that was made. In him was life; and the life was the light of men. And the light shineth in darkness; and the darkness comprehended it not.
- John 1:1-5 (KJV)

Jesus was the Word that became flesh and dwelt among us. He is the light that gets rid of the shadows in our identities.

The lens is light and easy. Jesus reminds us in Matthew 11:23 that His yoke is easy and his burden is light. So, even though, upon using this lens, it will take some more work to get our identities the way they should be, it's not hard because Christ has already paid the price. It doesn't mean we won't have to make adjustments. As we continuously view ourselves through the lens of the Word, we will always be making adjustments. The job of the light is to drive out the darkness. There are some views we have of ourselves that are dark, and they need to be eradicated with the light of the Word.

We didn't have to pay for the lens because the price was paid when Jesus died on the Cross. Our new identity was paid in full with His shed blood. We don't have to do anything to earn it. We just have to accept it and begin to see ourselves through His eyes.

When we read the Word and get an understanding of how God sees us, we are able to come into our identity with confidence. We have to meditate on the Word and begin to discern what it is God wants us to know about ourselves. As we discover who we are in Christ, we are in a better position to understand the heart of our Father.

As we consistently meditate on the Word as Joshua 1:8 commands us, we rehearse the things God has said and when negative thoughts attempt to arise, we counteract them with the Word. If you try to counteract negative thoughts without weapons, you are going to get beat every time. The Word is a weapon to be used to defend against the attacks of the enemy. We use it to defend against 'stinkin' thinkin'.

When thoughts attempt to come up that shift our vision from what has been said and decreed, then we have the weapon of the Word to use as our defense. The Scripture that I always turn to during times like this can be found in 2 Corinthians 10:5. It states, "Casting down imaginations, and every high thing that exalts itself against the knowledge of God, and bringing into captivity every thought to the obedience of Christ."

The thing to note is that we cast down imaginations and high things. We are the ones who bring thoughts into captivity to the obedience of Christ. We may be standing around waiting for God to give us inside information on how to handle our thoughts, and He is waiting for us to take them into captivity. If it was His responsibility, He wouldn't have told us to do it.

This is how we deal with those labels and expectations that have been placed on us. We cast them down with the understanding that we are new creatures in Christ.

The world will constantly give us false examples of our identities. We should be like "so and so". We should have marriages like "___ and ___". The sad part is that depending on the day, anyone can be placed in the blank. God created us to be individuals, so why do we consistently feel the need to be like everyone else? I understand

> **God in His infinite wisdom created YOU exactly like He wanted, so stop trying to change who you are!!!**

being different is against the norm. Think about if Jesus went with the norm and didn't dare to be different. Where would we be? What about the disciples? The early church? We would have no idea who we were supposed to be because we would be spending all of our time being like everyone else. God in His infinite wisdom created YOU exactly like He wanted, so stop trying to change who you are!!!

There are times when we try so hard to fit in when the word of God clearly tells us we are not to be conformed to this world, but be transformed by the renewing of our minds. We are a peculiar people. We are set apart. The only place we should be trying to fit in is the Body of Christ.

In 2 Corinthians 12, it says we are the body of Christ, who God has fitly joined together and that every joint supplies according to the need of the Body. So don't spend so much time trying to figure out how to fit in. Instead, spend time finding your purpose and place in the Body of Christ.

Take Away
I choose to view myself through the lens of the Word and not the lens of the World.

Practical Application
How can I identify the areas that I need to focus on through the lens of the Word vs. the lens of the World? With the help of the Word, how can I pinpoint them?

_____

_____

_____

_____

_____

_____

_____

_____

_____

Unveiling Your True Identity

Authentically You

Chapter 7
Saying What God Says (Say What?)

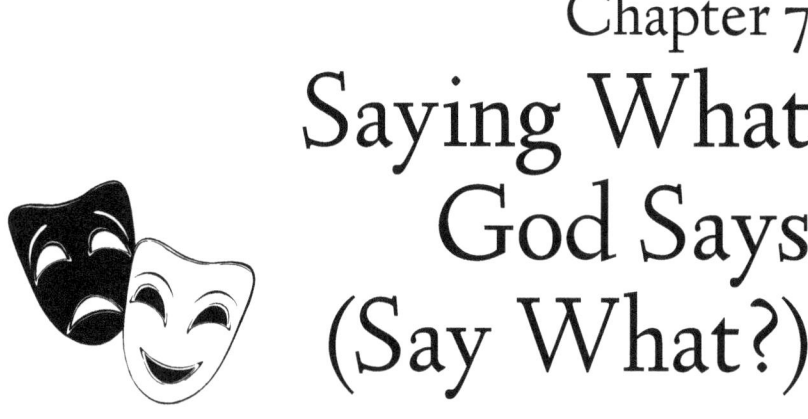

The final way to claim our identity is by saying what God has said about us. There are times when we may feel that our voice isn't necessary, and it doesn't matter. In this chapter, we are going to discuss why this is a lie and why the enemy doesn't want us to grab ahold of the knowledge that our voice is vitally important to establishing and maintaining our identity.

The word 'say', as defined in Merriam-Webster Online Dictionary, means to use your voice to express (something) with words; to express (an opinion); to express (a fact) with certainty. When I read this definition, I almost threw a shoe because it adds so much validity to the importance of our words. There is nothing on this earth more powerful than the words that come out of our mouths. We can use them to either build or destroy; the decision is ours. What we have to understand is that once they are uttered, we can never take them back.

There is a story floating around on social media about a teacher who used a powerful illustration to reinforce this to her students. She had several students grab tubes of various substances and squeeze out everything within the tube, things such as toothpaste, glue, gel, etc. After they emptied the containers, she instructed them to put it back in the tube. Of course, this was not feasible. The point she effectively made was that just like the substances in the tube could not be put back in after it came out, so are our words, once spoken. We cannot undo something we have said.

This is why what we say about ourselves matters. If we constantly say negative words, then that is what we hear all of the time. If we aren't quick to change the words, there will come a time when we don't even realize that every word coming out of our mouths is pessimistic. If we are always putting ourselves down, consistently telling ourselves we aren't good at this or that, then eventually we will believe it.

> **There is nothing on this earth more powerful than the words that come out of our mouths.**

The Bible states that as a man thinks in his heart, so is he. What we say has a lot to do with what we think. People typically don't speak without thinking about what they are going to say, (I said typically).

So, whatever we are meditating on is what is in our heart, and it will usually come out in what we say. Are we saying what God says about us or are we rehearsing what other people have said about us? We have to hold those thoughts and words up to the mirror of the Word to see if we need to change the words that are coming out of our mouth.

> *But be ye doers of the word, and not hearers only, deceiving your own selves. For if any be a hearer of the word, and not a doer, he is like unto a man beholding his natural face in a glass: For he beholdeth himself, and goeth his way, and straightway forgetteth what manner of man he was. But whoso looketh into the perfect law of liberty, and continueth therein, he being not a forgetful hearer, but a doer of the work, this man shall be blessed in his deed.*
> James 1:22-25 (KJV)

James admonishes us to not only be hearers of the Word, but doers as well. Don't just "hear" what you are reading, but actually practically apply what you have read. This is why we have the practical applications in this book. When we only "hear" and don't "do", we lie to ourselves. James said we are like a person who looks in a mirror who sees himself and once he leaves out of the mirror, he promptly forgets everything he has seen. Without practical application, there will be no lasting change. We look. We see. We walk away and wonder what happened. We are trying to figure out why we haven't seen change. We haven't done anything to see it. Our mouths are silent, and we haven't given voice to what's going on.

Silence is just as deafening as speaking negativity, if not more so. By not saying anything, we unconsciously agree with every thought that may come into our head. Silence doesn't bring about change. If anything when we are silent, it seems as if we are accepting and agreeing with what is being said. At times, when we are at work someone may say something we don't particularly agree with and instead of debating or getting into an argument, we stay silent. Usually, the person takes the silence as agreement and keeps talking. They don't recognize that we aren't saying anything back and until we speak up, they will continue to take our silence as agreement.

The enemy is no different. When we don't address with our words the things he is saying about us, it seems like we are in agreement with it. We choose to accept it because we haven't said otherwise. A believer without a voice is like living on a street without an address.

> *Bless the Lord, ye his angels,*
> *that excel in strength, that do his commandments,*
> *hearkening unto the voice of his word*
> Psalms 103:20 (KJV)

Silence in the kingdom of heaven doesn't guarantee a delivery. It says that the angels of the Lord hearkened unto the voice of his Word. If we aren't speaking the Word, our angels have no way to do His commandments. They are angels without an assignment.

If God used words to create the universe and everything within it, why do we believe that our words are not important? God called those things that be not as though they were until they became. God used the power of His words and His voice to create. We are made in His image and likeness; we have the power to create with our words as well.

When it comes to our identity, the power of confession is vitally important. James 3:5, 8-10 says, "the tongue is a little member, and it can boast of great things. See how much wood or how great a forest a tiny spark can set ablaze! But the human tongue can be tamed by no man. It is a restless (undisciplined, irreconcilable) evil, full of deadly poison. With it we bless the Lord and Father, and with it we curse men who were made in God's likeness! Out of the same mouth come forth blessing and cursing. These things, my brethren, ought not to be so."

Our tongue can be used to bless God, esteem Him, worship Him, exalt and honor Him, and then it can turn around and be self-destructing. We begin talking bad about ourselves. We are blessing God and cursing ourselves, and that shouldn't be. We need to remember who we are in Christ and begin to say what God has said about us.

He has called us His sons and daughters and said that He will be a Father to us (2 Corinthians 6:18). He told us that we can ask anything in His name, and He would do it. We can't ask without using our voice. Our words have the power to shape our future, and we have to make sure that we are saying what He has said.

When we have problems submitting to the Word and seeing ourselves the way God sees us, we resolve the problem by saying what He has said about us.

> I am a child of God (John 1:12)
> I am secure in Christ (John 10:27-29
> I am reigning in life through Jesus Christ (Rom. 5:17)
> I am free from condemnation. (Romans 8:1)
> I am complete in Christ (Colossians 2:7)
> I cannot be separated from the love of God (Rom. 8:11)
> I am a new creature. (2 Corinthians 5:17)
> I am redeemed from the hands of the enemy. (Psa 107:2)
> I am seated in heavenly places (Ephesians 2:6)
> I am an heir according to the promise. (Galatians 3:29)
> I am fearfully and wonderfully made (Psa. 139:14)
> I have a future and an expected end (Jeremiah 29:11)

What have we been saying about ourselves? Does what we say line up with what God has said? The list above is just a few of the things God has said about us and our identity. True identity is found in Christ and in order for us to succeed in life and to fulfill our purpose, we must be confident in who God created us to be. We cannot shy away from our assignment because we are unsure of who we are. We have the Word of God as our foundation.

Take Away
I have to say what God says about me. I cannot allow my voice to remain silent.

Practical Application
Write a confession about who you are in Christ based upon the Word and say it every day for the next thirty days.

Unveiling Your True Identity

Authentically You

PART III
IDENTITY CRISIS: AVERTED

Authentically You

Chapter 8
Confidence

In Part Three, we will discuss three things we gain that assist in averting an identity crisis. What do I mean by averting an identity crisis? I'm talking about preventing and warding it off. It is time to stop this crisis that plagues the lives of so many.

In John 17, Jesus prayed to the Father regarding the disciples. He prayed they would be unified, and they would be kept from evil. He also prayed they would be sanctified through the truth of the Word. He said that they were not of this world, just like He was not of this world. They were to be sent into the world. Just like the disciples, we are called to be in the world and not of the world. We have a different residence, and we are representatives of God. As such, we need to be confident in who we are just as much as we are confident in who we represent.

Confidence is defined, according to the Free Dictionary, as a belief or conviction that an outcome will be favorable; belief in the certainty of something; belief in the effectiveness of one's own abilities or in one's favorable acceptance by others; self-confidence; trust or faith in a person or thing; a trusting relationship.

We have to have faith that who God has created us to be is exactly who we need to be in order to be sent into the world. When Christ redeemed mankind back into relationship with God, mankind's confidence was restored. Our trust in God and God's trust in us was reestablished.

We know we can stand on the promises of God and expect them to come to pass. We should have an unshakeable faith in who God created us to be. Our confidence isn't tied to our education, our experiences, or any other external thing. Our confidence is tied to the Word of God.

> **Our confidence is tied to the Word of God.**

The Word of God is where we place our faith. If God has said it about us, we have to decide to believe it. Confidence is a conviction that an outcome will be favorable, in spite of what it may look like. We can either trust God and our relationship with Him, or we can base our confidence on other people's words, thoughts, and opinions.

Jesus was very confident in who He was. People questioned him every time they had an opportunity. People will do the same with us. Why are you doing that? Are you sure it is the right thing to do? What if it doesn't work out? What happens if you "miss" it?

Like Christ, we have to make sure we are doing and saying what the Father has said and done. People will always look for an opportunity to question who we say we are and what we believe about ourselves. At the end of the day, our confidence doesn't come from others. We have to be careful not to seek the "approval" of man and instead seek the approval of God. God will ask us to give an account for what He has instructed us to do, not what other people thought we should have done.

There is a confidence that comes from knowing who you are. Once you have a solid belief of your true identity, no one will be able to steer you away from that. Someone told me once that I didn't know who I was because I didn't act like a particular person. Can you say fumes? I was so angry. I almost went off on them. In the end, I walked away and didn't respond to the comment. I knew that I didn't have to prove myself to anyone. Craziness. After that interaction, I looked at the person differently because I didn't understand how they could want me to behave like someone else when I wasn't that person. I went to God and asked Him if He was okay with me. He reassured me that I was fine and I was becoming exactly who He created me to be.

You see, it took me a long time to develop my confidence in Christ, and it is an ongoing process. In every new season of our lives, not only do we learn something new about ourselves, but we also we have to develop the confidence needed to uphold our identity. When we spend so many years living for the approval of others and accepting the labels and unrealistic expectations of them, finding our confidence in Christ will become a process. Who we really are doesn't appear overnight. It takes constantly renewing our mind, meditating on the Word, and spending time with God to regain our confidence. Once we regain our confidence, it is easy to stand up to the people who try to force us to be something or someone we aren't.

Jesus' confidence didn't come from pleasing others. It came from pleasing the Father. After Christ was baptized, it says in Matthew 3:17 a voice from heaven said, "This is my beloved Son, in whom I am well pleased". We should have the same attitude and desire for God to say the same thing about us. "This is my beloved Son or Daughter, in whom I am well pleased." We please God when we have faith in who He created us to be. We don't have to be who others want us to be in order to please them. We have to be who God created us to be in order to please God. In every season of our lives, God will ask us to do something that is outside of our comfort zone. In each season, He is providing us with a new part of our identity, and we will have to develop our confidence in that area.

Have you ever lost confidence in yourself? Or your abilities? Or some skills that you had at one point in your life? I believe we have all been there. We have looked in the mirror and questioned why we look the way we do. Sometimes, it may even pop up during the time you are thinking about that position that you really want. You can begin to feel inferior. You can start to question your ability to do the job even though you know you have the knowledge and skills to be successful in that position. Guess what? It can even show up while talking to a friend, relative, or someone from church. It's a lie from the enemy himself that tells us we aren't worthy and that we don't deserve it, whatever 'it' may be. Why are you second guessing your right to be you and who God created you to be? It's about being confident in the skin you are in for every area of your life.

I was invited to join a mastermind group of Christian women who are entrepreneurs. Now to be completely open I was surprised at first. These women were and still are movers and shakers in their own right. To say I was intimidated is an understatement. I had just started my business and I wasn't quite sure where it was going. I was in the middle of planning a wedding, and I felt like I didn't quite belong. In my mind, I was nowhere near their level.

There were times when I would tell my husband how I didn't want to go to dinner with them because I didn't feel like I deserved to be there. This feeling of inadequacy showed up every time we were going to meet. Finally, my husband asked me, "What are you afraid of? Why are you intimidated? Either accept your place at the table or decline the invite. We will not go through this every time you guys have a plan to meet." I had to take a very hard look at myself and ask

God why I felt this way. Finally, the answer came. FEAR. I was afraid to fail and not live up to their expectations. I decided to push past my initial reservations and continue to meet with them.

Two years later, we still meet to talk about our businesses, where we are, where God is taking us and what our next steps are along the journey. I realized the only expectation they had of me was to be myself. It is partially because of this group that you are reading this book. The other is my husband. I had to give him a shout out. We have encouraged, supported, and cheered each other on even in the midst of challenges. Had I let this lack of confidence and self-worth and the thought that I had nothing to bring to the table stop me from participating in this group, I'm not sure if anyone would ever be reading this book.

In order to become great, you need to be around someone else who is becoming great.
– Pastor Sean R. Moore

The relationships that God has ordained in our lives will challenge us. They should challenge us. If they don't, then we need to reevaluate those relationships. Every relationship is not supposed to make us feel great. Some of those relationships are supposed to get us out of our comfort zone. The support and the accountability is there to assist us in becoming our best. It is so much easier to see the greatness in others than it is to see in ourselves. That is why God has us in relationships with people we may have never chosen if it was up to us at that given time. Thank God for His divine set ups.

We have to be careful not to let our fear and lack of confidence talk us out of feeling like we belong. I had briefly mentioned to the ladies that I didn't feel like I belonged, but I never opened up to them completely. I didn't need them to reassure me, although that would have been great for my ego. I needed to go to the source...God. A good friend reminded me not to reject what God has placed on the inside of me. The only person who can make us feel inadequate is the person we're looking at in the mirror. When we lack confidence in any area, we have to figure out why. God has never made anything with a deficiency, including us. Stand with confidence in the identity you've been given.

Take away
Don't let your own lack of confidence stop you from accessing and fully participating in the relationships that God has designed for you to fulfill your purpose.

Practical Application
What is one thing I can do, even if it may be uncomfortable, to position myself for God ordained relationships in my life?

_____
_____
_____
_____
_____
_____
_____
_____
_____
_____
_____
_____

Unveiling Your True Identity

Authentically You

Chapter 9
Rights and Benefits

When Jesus died on the cross and rose from the dead, He redeemed man. He restored us back to our original status. One of the definitions of restore, according to Merriam-Webster Dictionary, is to return something to an earlier or original condition by repairing it, cleaning it; to give back something that was lost or taken, to put or bring something back into existence or use. When I read this definition, I almost jumped out of my seat.

This is exactly what Christ did for man. He returned us back to our original condition by repairing our relationship with God. Our original condition is found in Genesis 1:26 "And God said, let us make man in our own image and likeness". Sound familiar? HELLO IDENTITY! Our identity was restored when Christ redeemed man.

One of my favorite things to talk about are the rights and benefits we have in Christ. When we apply for a job, nine times out of ten, we look at the benefits package. We think about the rewards. The benefits package may include salary, medical benefits, dental benefits, vision, holidays, the amount of personal and sick time we accrue per pay period.

Well, guess what? We have benefits and rights once our identity has been restored in Christ. This new identity grants us access in the Kingdom. How often are we unaware of what we actually have access to and as a result we accept anything that comes our way?

> *But when the right time came, God sent His Son, who was born from a woman and lived under the law. God did this so that He could buy the freedom of those who were under the law. God's purpose was to make us his children. Since you are now God's children, He has sent the Spirit of his Son into your hearts. The Spirit cries out, "Abba, Father. Now you are not slaves like before. You are God's children, and you will receive everything He promised his children.*
> *Galatians 4:4-7 (ERV)*

Notice it says that because we are God's children, we will receive everything that He promised us. This is great news. Here is proof that we have access to God's promises as His children.

My previous company paid for all of the benefits for the single employees. When I say all, I mean all. There were no deductions from my paycheck for any benefits. Ask me how many times I utilized those benefits in two years? NEVER!!! I didn't notice that they were available. Unbelievable, right? Yeah, I realized that after I left. How many of us do that with the benefits we receive as children of God?

We don't even realize we have full access to every benefit afforded to Christ. Before I knew who I was in Christ, I just accepted whatever. No more!! We have rights as the King's kids. We have to choose to use and accept them all.

Let's look at some of the rights and benefits we have as a result of finding our identity in Christ. We have been given authority and dominion on the earth. We have been promised healing. We have been promised wholeness. We have been promised Holy Spirit. We have been promised access to the throne of God. These are just a few of the promises given to us.

Before Adam and Eve ate of the tree of knowledge of good and evil, God gave them dominion over the earth.

"...and let them have complete authority over the fish of the sea, the birds of the air, the [tame] beasts, and over all of the earth, and over everything that creeps upon the earth.
So God created man in His own image, in the image and likeness of God He created him; male and female He created them.
And God blessed them and said to them, Be fruitful, multiply, and fill the earth,

and subdue it [using all its vast resources in the service of God and man]; and have dominion over the fish of the sea, the birds of the air, and over every living creature that moves upon the earth"
Genesis 1:26-28 (AMP)

That sounds like authority and dominion to me. This is our first identity. If the labels and names that we were called does not line up with our identity that has been restored through Christ, we do not have to accept it. The revelation of understanding our authority and dominion on earth is the foundation to accessing the other benefits we have in Christ.

Healing is a promise to the believer. One of the assignments of Jesus was to heal the broken hearted. Isaiah 53:5 says "...and with his stripes we are healed." I Peter 2:24 states "...by whose stripes ye were healed." We have a right to healing in Christ. We have to exercise faith and understand our authority. When we don't feel well or symptoms attempt to attack our bodies, we have to utilize our authority over our bodies. Please do not get me wrong. If you are taking medication under the advisement of a physician, do not stop taking it without the approval of your doctor.

There have been times where my body has experienced symptoms. I do things in the natural (rest, orange juice, going to the doctor, etc.) I also attack it in the spirit through prayer and my confession. What we say about ourselves as it relates to the promises of God is so very important.

In John 10:10, Christ promised us that He came so that we may have and enjoy life, and have it in abundance (to the full, till it overflows.) The abundant life is the God kind of life. It's the life we receive after accepting Christ. He gives us joy, peace, patience, meekness, gentleness, and most importantly love. This life promises wholeness and completeness in Christ. The result of this benefit is rooted in our becoming new creatures in Christ. It speaks to the identity we have, not the identity we lost. We are complete and whole in Christ. We do not need anyone to complete us.

> **We are complete and whole in Christ.**

When we understand that we don't need anyone else to complete us, our relationships take on an entirely different perspective. We don't have to subject ourselves to toxic friends and family members in order to feel accepted. We don't have to be involved with the opposite sex to feel validated. Christ has already accepted and validated us. There is no need to jump from one relationship to another, looking for something undefinable. When we seek completion outside of Christ, we haven't gotten a true understanding of our identity in Him.

We have access to the throne of God. Hebrews 4:16 says, "Let us then fearlessly and confidently and boldly draw near to the throne of grace (the throne of God's unmerited favor to us sinners), that we may receive mercy [for our failures] and find grace to help in good time for every need [appropriate help and well-timed help, coming just when we need it." (AMP)

We can approach the throne of God with boldness and confidence without fear. It is there we receive God's grace and mercy. As a teenager/young adult, I did not have to ask permission to come into my home. I had access via a key. We don't have to ask permission to enter the throne of God, like the priest in the Old Testament. We have a key (Jesus) that gives us access to the Father.

God is a good God and provides good gifts to His children. The best gift we have received after salvation is the gift of Holy Spirit. When God said He would never leave us or forsake us, He knew we would have Holy Spirit living within us. Jesus sent the disciples to Jerusalem to wait in the upper room for Holy Spirit to fall upon them. When we accept Jesus, Holy Spirit comes to live within us for the development of our character. When we receive the promise of Holy Spirit upon us, it is for power. Jesus' ministry did not begin until He had been baptized and Holy Spirit descended upon Him like a dove.

Holy Spirit allows us to access the other benefits mentioned in this chapter. There is a boldness and a confidence that we have as children when we know that God did not leave us by ourselves to live the life of a Christian. He sent us help.

Every believer has this new identity in Christ and access to all of the promises mentioned. When a package is delivered that we didn't order, we typically go into super stealth mode trying to figure out where it came from. The same can be done in the spirit. I am quick to say that something isn't a part of my benefits package because I know who I am and whose I am. If it is not something promised by God, then we have no obligation to receive it. It has to be returned to the sender. Why would we take something that isn't ours even if it is sent to us? Send it back and stand on the promises of God.

My husband and I are going through some physical challenges. We found a Scripture that speaks to our situation, and we are standing on the promises of God. We are fully persuaded in knowing that God is able to do exactly what He promised, and we will not be moved until we see the manifestation in the natural. So, when our bodies don't want to cooperate, we remember we have access to the throne and benefits as His children. We have no problem returning the package to the sender.

Whatever the situation may be, we need to know that we have been restored to our original state before the fall. We have full access to the promises of God. It is time we started behaving like it. We can't let the enemy be a spiritual bully in our lives. He comes to steal, kill, and destroy. That's his job. This doesn't mean that we have to let him steal our lunch money. We have all of heaven standing behind us. There are so many times where we just accept what he does in our lives, and then we try to play the victim. We give him too much credit. Greater is He that is in me (us) than he that is in the world. We have to stop being spiritual cowards and become intimately acquainted with what has been promised to us. When we have a full revelation of this, we won't have a problem standing up to the enemy and reminding him of who we are. Our identity allows us to stand firm on the Word of God as we utilize all that God has for us.

Take Away
As a child of the Most High God, I have access to benefits of the kingdom.

Practical Application
How can I find the other promises God made to His children and apply them in my life?

_____

_____

_____

_____

_____

_____

_____

_____

_____

_____

_____

Authentically You

Chapter 10
Crisis AVERTED

When we are confident in who we are and understand our rights and benefits as children of God, it makes fulfilling our purpose on the earth easier. We won't be moved by people's thoughts, opinions, or ideas about what we should be doing. When God has given us an assignment, we understand that we can't complete it without His help. We also realize that we need to know who we are in Christ. Otherwise, we will sit and wait for it to be done by someone else.

The confidence that comes from knowing who we are is immeasurable. We won't be moved or swayed by our own thinking. Instead we move forward knowing that God has equipped us with

> **We have been called to greatness.**

everything we need in order to get the job done. I'm not saying that we won't have moments where we pause and say, "Really, God? You want me to do what?" However, after that moment, we will get ourselves together and remember that to whom much is given, much is required.

Sometimes we need a quick reminder, and that is where our "team" comes in. These are the people who God has placed in our lives to be our cheerleaders and our accountability partners. These are the people who tell us when we need to get it together and make it happen. If you don't have a "team", I encourage you to pray and ask God to send them to you. We ultimately have Holy Spirit living on the inside of us reminding us we have been called to greatness.

When we don't know our identity, we struggle with fulfilling purpose. We struggle to find the confidence to complete the assignment we have been tasked with as Christ's representatives on earth. One of my favorite passages of Scripture about this subject is John 21:3-18. Prior to this Scripture, Jesus gave the disciples instructions to go to Jerusalem and wait for the Holy Spirit. Once they received the gift of Holy Spirit, they would have power to be witnesses in Jerusalem, Judea, Samaria, and the uttermost part of the earth (Acts 1:8).

> **Greatness exists outside of our comfort zone.**

The instructions were simple to follow. Go. Wait. Receive. Be a witness. It doesn't get any simpler than that. However, Peter made a decision to go fishing and six of the disciples decided to go with him. In my own opinion, Peter had an identity crisis. He completely forgot who he was, what he had been exposed to (Christ), his purpose (building the church), and went back to his comfort zone. How many times has God called us out of our comfort zone to do something great for Him, but because we waver in who we are, we pass on the opportunity?

Greatness exists outside of our comfort zone. We cannot fulfill our purpose on the earth without knowing who we are in Christ. When we have an identity crisis, we can lead people away from their purpose. This is exactly what Peter did when he went back to his fishing business and took the other disciples with him. None of them were in the place they were supposed to be or doing what they were instructed to do.

How many people are in this same situation because they are having an identity crisis? There are people who are waiting for us to step into our identity because we have what they need. God is not asking us to be someone we aren't to meet their needs. He is asking us to be ourselves because we have something they need on the inside of us.

While in Bible school, I was working for a non-profit organization part time. My immediate supervisor was leaving the company and wanted me to apply for the position. In my heart, I knew that I was not sent to the company to occupy that position. My supervisor insisted that I apply. I found out they were conducting interviews during the time we were having Youth Camp. I was not willing to sacrifice attending Youth Camp to interview for a position I was not suppose to take. My supervisor was visibly upset and didn't understand my decision. At the end of the day, I didn't feel an explanation was necessary. Later in the year, I left the company and began working for another organization that gave me flexibility. I ended up serving in a different capacity, which turned out to be a part of my preparation for my purpose.

If I would have given in to the pressure to apply for that position, I would have been like Peter on the boat fishing when I should have been somewhere else. I was confident in knowing God did not want me in the position because I knew who I was in Christ. I was free from public opinion, and I understood not everyone would understand my assignment. I was ok with it all. People will attempt to tell us what they think is best for us and get upset when we decide not to do what they want.

God knows what is best for us. We have to be firmly persuaded that He has our best interest at heart. He is not going to lead us into a ditch as long as we are following Him. Minister Minyon Brooks said, "God will always protect the integrity of our heart." That statement set me free from wondering what would happen if I "missed" it.
If we believe that we are being obedient to what God has said and we "miss" it, then He will honor our heart. He looks at the heart

of a person. We can't get caught up in "what if I miss it or what if I'm wrong or what if I didn't hear God". A double minded man is unstable in all his ways (James 1:8).

We become paralyzed with fear about not getting it exactly right. We have to move forward in faith and know that God has got our back. Remember, fear gets to the edge of the cliff and says 'what if' while faith gets to the edge of the cliff and says 'God's got this'. Let's be moved by faith and not by fear.

> *God will anoint you to serve someone else.*
> *He will not anoint you to become someone else.*
> **– Pastor Sean R. Moore**

God is not asking us to be someone else. He expects us to be ourselves and to use the gifts and talents He has given us to move the Kingdom forward. We don't see God's other creations trying to be something they are not. The mountains aren't crashing down into the sea trying to be a fish. The birds aren't trying to be a river. The sunset isn't trying to be the sunrise. Each of these things understand what they are in creation and glorify God exactly the way they have been designed.

I understand they are inanimate objects, but have you ever seen the beauty of a sunset or sunrise over the ocean? That image glorifies God and no two sunsets and sunrises are ever the same. God has not asked us to be chameleons, where we change everything about us in order to be someone He hasn't anointed us to be. Chameleons blend in so well with their surroundings other animals don't even know they are there. Have we blended in so well with the world that people don't even know we are believers? Have we blended in so well that we have lost who we are? God has called us to stand out.

In 1 Peter 1:9 it says that we are a chosen generation, a royal priesthood, a holy nation, and a peculiar people. It says that we should show forth the praises of him who has called us out of darkness into His marvelous light. The time for hiding is over. We have been called out of darkness into God's marvelous light. Our identity in Christ is crucial to the people who need the light.

For I reckon that the sufferings of this present time are not worthy to be compared with the glory which shall be revealed in us. For the earnest expectation of the creature waiteth for the manifestation of the sons of God.
Romans 8:18-19 (KJV)

What we go through as Believers in this life is nothing compared to the glory that will be revealed in us when we finally see Jesus. However, while we are waiting for that day, the earth cries out for the manifestation of the sons of God. The earth cries out for those who are Believers. We are the ones who know our identity. And just like the earth cries out, how many souls are waiting for us to step into our identity so that we can walk in our purpose? Remember the earnest expectation is there. When do we rise up to meet this expectation?

This is an expectation that God has placed on the Believer. This is not an unrealistic expectation. We have to do our part and do it with a confidence that cannot be deterred by others. Most importantly, we have to stay confident even when the pessimism is self-imposed. We can't talk ourselves out of completing the assignment that God has given us to fulfill in and on the earth.

There was a confidence that Jesus had because He knew who He was and who sent him. Jesus was very clear in that he did not do anything outside of what God had instructed Him to do. In John 5:19, Jesus stated "Truly, truly, I say to you, the Son can do nothing of his own accord, but only what he sees the Father doing. For whatever the Father does, that the Son does likewise." (ESV). When Christ performed miracles, He didn't hesitate. He knew what had to be done, and He did it.

As we live day by day, we have to ask ourselves if we are doing what God has instructed us to do. Are we living our purpose? Are we saying what God has said? When we are, we can rest assured God and all of heaven is backing us up. We can have that same confidence because we know who we are and who we represent. We have access to the rights and benefits that come from being His children. We use the authority and dominion we have been given to decree and declare the Word of God. The power that we have when we know who we are in the Word cannot be taken away from us; however, we can give that power away by being less than who God created us to be. It is time for us to walk in our God given identity, unapologetic and unashamed. The decision is ours.

Take away
When we are confident in our identity, we can fulfill our God-given purpose.

Practical Application
What are some ways that I can build my confidence to fulfill my purpose on the earth?

_____

_____

_____

_____

_____

_____

_____

_____

_____

_____

_____

Prayer

The first step to becoming your authentic self is by establishing a relationship with Jesus Christ. I am not talking about a religion, but a relationship. It is one of the easiest things to do. If you would like to have a relationship, read this prayer below out loud believe it in your heart, and you will be saved.

Father, in the name of Jesus, I believe that Jesus is the Son of God. I believe He died for my sins, and is risen from the dead. I am a sinner in need of a Savior. I confess with my mouth and believe with my heart that Jesus is Lord. I accept him as my Lord, Savior, and Master. Father, thank you for making me your child and giving me a new idenitity. I am now saved. In Jesus' Name. Amen

Welcome to the family!!!

Resources

National Suicide Prevention Lifeline
1 (800) 273-8255
www.suicidepreventionlifeline.org

Prayer Hotline
24 Hour Prayer: 800-541-7729 (PRAY)

Merriam-Webster. Merriam-Webster. Web. 23 Aug. 2015.
www.merriam-webster.com

Dictionary, Encyclopedia and Thesaurus. The Free Dictionary. Farlex. Web. 23 Aug. 2015.
www.thefreedictionary.com

Acknowledgements

It can be easy to overlook the people who have helped you become who you are, this is my attempt. If I have left anyone out, please charge it to my head and not my heart. Thank you for taking this journey with me.

First of all, to Lawrence, thank you for your commitment to see me do and be my best. Not just as a wife and friend, but as a daughter of the King. Thank you for pushing me to be all that God has destined me to be. #TeamRiddick for life

To my parents, family, and friends that are like family, thank you for your love, prayers, and unwavering support.

To the Pastors and Staff of Faith Christian Center Phoenix, Impact Church Jacksonville, and Impact Church Central Florida, there are no words that can adequately explain how much I love you all. Thank you for believing in me, supporting me, and most of all letting me be me.

To my Accountability Partners – IC, AG, OF, EA, and MS – thank you for the texts, the check-ups, the follow ups, and most of all the laughs.

To Mag 6 – No words, absolutely no words. I will not cry.

To my editor, Darrian Tanner, who knew that a divine connection while living in Orlando would lead to one of the greatest relationships I would need four years later? God did. Thank you for your time, talent and patience. It has been God-ordained since Chapter 1.

And last but not least, to the Best Father a girl could ask for…Thank you God for trusting me to be a vessel to your people. I am humbled at the responsibility. My prayer has been and will always be I decrease as you increase. Here is your servant, send me Lord, send me. May people's lives be forever changed because you trusted me.

www.ingramcontent.com/pod-product-compliance
Lightning Source LLC
Chambersburg PA
CBHW060200050426
42446CB00013B/2913